This Journal
Belongs To:

Made in the
USA
Monee, IL

15427896R00069